HOW TO BUILD
GREAT RELATIONSHIPS

PRINCIPLES FOR
FRIENDSHIP AND PARTNERSHIP,
MARRIAGE AND PARENTING

HOW TO BUILD
GREAT RELATIONSHIPS

PRINCIPLES FOR
FRIENDSHIP AND PARTNERSHIP,
MARRIAGE AND PARENTING

BRIAN HOUSTON

PUBLISHED BY MAXIMISED LEADERSHIP

How to build great relationships
First published July 2002

Copyright © 2002 Brian Houston
All rights reserved. No part of this publication may be reproduced
in any form or by any means without prior written permission from
the publisher.

> Houston, Brian
> ISBN 0 9577336 7 4

Scripture quotations used in this book are from the following
sources and used with permission:
New King James Version (NKJV). Copyright © 1982, 1992 by
Thomas Nelson, Inc. Used by permission. All rights reserved.
The Amplified Bible (AMP). Old Testament Copyright ©
1965,1987 by the Zondervan Corporation. New Testament
Copyright © 1958, 1987 by the Lockman Foundation. Used by
permission.

Bold emphasis in certain scriptures is the author's own.

Back cover photo of Brian and Bobbie Houston by Femia Shirtliff

Printed by Emerald Press, Castle Hill NSW Australia

Published by Maximised Leadership,
PO Box 1195, Castle Hill, NSW 1765 Australia

DEDICATION

BUILDING GREAT RELATIONSHIPS

Two are better than one, because they have a good reward for their labour. For if they fall, one will lift up his companion. But woe to him who is alone when he falls, for he has no one to help him up. Again, if two lie down together, they will keep warm; but how can one be warm alone? Though one may be overpowered by another, two can withstand him. And a threefold cord is not quickly broken.

One of the greatest gifts God has given us is people. When you think of giving someone gifts, you may think of inanimate objects or things, but God thinks of people. When He saw Adam was alone, He gave him a wife and companion. When He saw the world in need, He gave us Jesus. When He wants to change an enterprise, community or nation, He raises up people who will fulfil His purposes.

Great relationships are a sign of a prosperous life but they don't come by chance. Sadly, we live in a world filled with broken relationships. I'm not only talking about broken marriages, but failed friendships, family fall-outs or bitter business partnerships. The reality is that you certainly don't fluke a good marriage, a great friendship or a successful business partnership. The principles that you sow into the relationship will determine what you reap.

Many take their relationships for granted and only when they experience problems, do they desperately seek answers or help. The truth is that if the pain and bitterness of one bad relationship is never dealt with, it has the potential to affect other relationships too. Yet the good news is that even those who have been hurt in intimate relationships can apply biblical principles, lay the right kind of foundations and go on to build great relationships.

So you want to know *how* to build great relationships? The Bible is the most comprehensive manual or handbook we have that contains all the principles we need for building successful relationships in every level of life. The Bible speaks about marriage, friendship, parenting, employer relations, leadership, how to treat others ... and how to have a great relationship with God Himself.

friendship

Greater love has no one than this, than to lay down one's life for his friends. You are My friends if you do whatever I command you. No longer do I call you servants, for a servant does not know what his master is doing; but I have called you friends, for all things that I heard from My Father I have made known to you.

THE POWER OF FRIENDSHIP

Greater love has no one than this, than to lay down one's life for his friends. You are My friends if you do whatever I command you. No longer do I call you servants, for a servant does not know what his master is doing; but I have called you friends, for all things that I heard from My Father I have made known to you.

TWO ARE BETTER THAN ONE, BECAUSE THEY HAVE A GO[OD] REWARD FOR THEIR LABOUR. FOR IF THEY FALL, ONE W[ILL] LIFT UP HIS COMPANION. BUT WOE TO HIM WHO IS ALO[NE] WHEN HE FALLS, FOR HAS NO ONE TO HELP HIM AGAIN, IF TWO LIE DOWN T[O]GETHER, THEY WILL KE[EP] WARM; BUT HOW CAN ONE BE WARM ALONE? THOUGH O[NE] MAY BE OVERPOWERED BY ANOTHER, TWO CAN WITHSTA[ND] HIM. AND A THREEFOLD CORD IS NOT QUICKLY BROKE[N]

> 'IT IS NOT GOOD THAT MAN SHOULD BE ALONE'
>
> [GENESIS 2:18]

LONELINESS

In the movie *Cast Away* actor Tom Hanks played a FedEx agent who was marooned on a remote Pacific island for four years. The need for friendship became so great that he kept himself sane by conversing with a basketball he named Wilson.

Solitary confinement is one of the harshest measures of punishment for an individual. Good, intimate relationships will build up our lives, whereas isolation will break us down. In the beginning, God said:

'It is not good that man should be alone.' [Genesis 2:18]

He created us to know the blessing of intimacy and within every one of us is the desire and need for companionship. Sadly, there are some who never seem to draw others into their lives. There is a proverb that says:

'A man who isolates himself seeks his own desire; he rages against all wise judgement.' [Proverbs 18:1]

This proverb describes a person who makes the choice to disconnect himself from others by 'seeking his own desire.' Instead of contributing to a relationship, such people are in it for their own gain, whether it be towards achieving a certain goal or needing constant approval and affirmation.

Why does such a person 'rage against all wise judgement'? People who are seeking their own desire inevitably make choices that support their particular pursuits. For example, someone who has an alcohol problem will gravitate towards drinking companions. Wise judgement would suggest that instead of relationships that support their weakness, they should seek to build friendships that strengthen and challenge them.

The starting point for building great relationships is making wise decisions about who we allow close to us. We need people who will build us up and take us forward, and good friends will do just that.

TWO ARE BETTER THAN ONE, BECAUSE THEY HAVE A GO[OD] REWARD FOR THEIR LABOUR. FOR IF THEY FALL, ONE W[ILL] LIFT UP HIS COMPANION. BUT WOE TO HIM WHO IS ALO[NE] WHEN HE FALLS, FOR HAS NO ONE TO HELP HIM AGAIN, IF TWO LIE DOWN T[O]GETHER, THEY WILL KE[EP] WARM; BUT HOW CAN ONE BE WARM ALONE? THOUGH O[NE] MAY BE OVERPOWERED BY ANOTHER, TWO CAN WITHSTA[ND] HIM. AND A THREEFOLD CORD IS NOT QUICKLY BROKE[N]

> 'A MAN WHO HAS FRIENDS MUST HIMSELF BE FRIENDLY'
>
> [PROVERBS 18:24]

BUILDING GREAT FRIENDSHIPS

Some of the most pleasurable moments in life are sitting around a table and sharing a meal with close friends. I'd consider friendship to be one of the key elements of a blessed life.

Thousands would crowd around Jesus to hear Him teach but it was His twelve companions who shared the most intimate moments of His life on earth. They were the ones who gathered together with Him in the upper room before His crucifixion, where He shared a table for twelve before the most challenging moment of His life.

The Bible says:

'A man who has friends must himself be friendly.' [Proverbs 18:24]

There are those who never attract others into their lives. They miss the blessing of friendship because their attitude is more about what they can *get* instead of what they can *give* into the relationship. Just as we need to make deposits before we make withdrawals from our bank accounts, so we need to invest into our relationships.

Another translation of Proverbs 18:24 illustrates a different aspect of friendship. It says:

'The man of many friends [a friend of all the world] will prove himself a bad friend.' [Proverbs 18:24 AMP]

There are many who want to be everyone's friend but they never become a true friend to anyone because they are not prepared to make a stand. Instead of giving a friend their whole-hearted support, they sit on the fence and try to be a friend to everyone.

A well-known personality in America who was sent to jail for his fraudulent activities was once asked if he had lost any friends. His answer was profound. He stated that he didn't lose any friends but he found out who his friends really were. A true friend will stick with you during the good times and the bad times.

TWO ARE BETTER THAN ONE, BECAUSE THEY HAVE A GO[OD]

REWARD FOR THEIR LABOUR. FOR IF THEY FALL, ONE W[ILL]

LIFT UP HIS COMPANION. BUT WOE TO HIM WHO IS ALO[NE]

WHEN HE FALLS, FOR [HE]

HAS NO ONE TO HELP HIM [UP.]

AGAIN, IF TWO LIE DOWN T[O-]

GETHER, THEY WILL KE[EP]

WARM; BUT HOW CAN ONE BE WARM ALONE? THOUGH O[NE]

MAY BE OVERPOWERED BY ANOTHER, TWO CAN WITHSTA[ND]

HIM. AND A THREEFOLD CORD IS NOT QUICKLY BROKE[N]

> 'GREATER LOVE HAS NO
> ONE THAN THIS,
> THAN TO LAY DOWN
> ONE'S LIFE
> FOR HIS FRIENDS.'
>
> [JOHN 15: 13]

LOYALTY AND LOVE

How far would you go for a friend who is in trouble? Napoleon Bonaparte once made this observation: 'Alexander, Caesar, Charlemagne and myself founded great empires, but upon which did the creations of our genius depend? Upon force! Jesus alone founded His empire upon love, and to this very day, millions would die for Him!'

Jesus said the following words:

'Greater love has no one than this, than to lay down one's life for His friends.' [John 15:13]

Jesus demonstrated His love by giving His life for us. He may have been betrayed by Judas, one of His twelve disciples, and Peter may have denied Him three times, but that didn't sway Him.

A friend is someone you love, and from whom you receive love. In ancient Greek and Latin, the word for *friend* ('philos' and 'amicus') is based on the word for *love* ('phile' and 'am').

The Bible describes a good friend in this way:

'A friend loves at all times.' [Proverbs 17:17]

Loyalty and love are the attributes of true friends. Such friends will be there in season and out of season. They are the ones who rejoice when you are rejoicing, and will weep when you are weeping. Your close friends will know your weaknesses and strengths, and they will have watched you make mistakes, but they will be there to see you through the times of adversity.

The strength of a good friendship that goes the distance will be unconditional love. Such people won't stand by and be neutral when they hear criticism or gossip by busybodies behind the back of their friend. Their loyalty will cause them to make a stand and if called for, they will even put their own reputation on the line. They will believe in you no matter what happens, and will be committed to seeing you reach your potential in life.

TWO ARE BETTER THAN ONE, BECAUSE THEY HAVE A GO

REWARD FOR THEIR LABOUR.   FOR IF THEY FALL, ONE W

LIFT UP HIS COMPANION. BUT WOE TO HIM WHO IS ALO

WHEN   HE   FALLS, FOR

> 'HE WHO WALKS WITH WISE MEN WILL BE WISE, BUT THE COMPANION OF FOOLS WILL BE DESTROYED'
>
> [PROVERBS 13:20]

HAS NO ONE   TO HELP HIM

AGAIN, IF TWO   LIE DOWN T

GETHER, THEY   WILL   KE

WARM; BUT HOW CAN ONE BE WARM ALONE? THOUGH O

MAY BE OVERPOWERED BY ANOTHER, TWO CAN WITHSTA

HIM. AND A THREEFOLD CORD IS NOT QUICKLY BROKE

A FRIEND TO YOUR DESTINY

Are your friends the kind of people who take you forward and build you up? Wisdom in choosing your friends enables you to build relationships with those who will lift you up and support you. You cannot expect to achieve your best in life without other people, but a true friend will be a friend to your destiny. The Bible warns us of friendships that are potentially destructive in our lives.

'*He who walks with wise men will be wise, but the companion of fools will be destroyed.*' [Proverbs 13:20]

As the saying goes, birds of a feather flock together, and you will find that like-minded people tend to gravitate towards each other. For instance, negativity breeds negativity, and such people seem to gravitate towards others with a similar cynical attitude.

The reality is that the mentality or attitude of those you hang around with eventually rubs off on you. The psalmist wrote:

'*I will set nothing wicked before my eyes; I hate the work of those who fall away; it shall not cling to me.*' [Psalm 101:3]

The spirit of those around you *will* stick to you like glue. Be careful of wrong associations and what you allow to cling to you. Not everyone who appears friendly is a friend. The Bible describes how Satan approached Jesus in the wilderness with a seemingly friendly attitude, yet he was obviously not a friend to the purposes of God. His motive was to tempt Jesus to abandon God's plan.

Yet good friends will have a positive influence in your life. There is a proverb that says:

'*As iron sharpens iron, so a man sharpens the countenance of his friend*' [Proverbs 27:17]

What rubs off on you will affect your future. Let the influence of your friends be one that sharpens and strengthens you the way iron sharpens iron.

TWO ARE BETTER THAN ONE, BECAUSE THEY HAVE A GO[OD]

REWARD FOR THEIR LABOUR. FOR IF THEY FALL, ONE W[ILL]

LIFT UP HIS COMPANION. BUT WOE TO HIM WHO IS ALO[NE]

WHEN HE FALLS, FOR [HE]

> 'FAITHFUL ARE THE
> WOUNDS OF
> A FRIEND'
>
> [PROVERBS 27:6]

HAS NO ONE TO HELP HIM [UP.]

AGAIN, IF TWO LIE DOWN T[O-]

GETHER, THEY WILL KE[EP]

WARM; BUT HOW CAN ONE BE WARM ALONE? THOUGH O[NE]

MAY BE OVERPOWERED BY ANOTHER, TWO CAN WITHSTA[ND]

HIM. AND A THREEFOLD CORD IS NOT QUICKLY BROKE[N.]

FRIENDLY ADVICE

Who do you turn to when you need good advice? In the same way that the spirit of your friends rubs off on you, so their counsel may cause you to make either good or bad decisions. A friend to your destiny is one who will sometimes tell you not what you *want* to hear but what you *need* to hear. The Bible says:

'Faithful are the wounds of a friend, but the kisses of an enemy are deceitful.' [Proverbs 27:6]

A friend will have the courage to be truthful with you, but always with your best interests at heart. When others may flatter you with compliments or cater to your sensitivities, a true friend will beautifully balance encouragement and honesty.

The suffering of the Old Testament character, Job, is well documented – he had lost his family, his fortune and his health. In the midst of it all, he was surrounded by counsel. There was his nagging wife and his three friends (or so-called comforters) who filled his ears with negativity and well-meaning advice. But Job refused to be swayed and firmly stood aloof from ungodly counsel. He spoke about:

'... when the friendly counsel of God was over my tent.' [Job 29:4]

The counsel of God is available to us through the Bible and will always be a friend to our destiny. There may be times when His counsel may not seem to be that friendly or favourable towards your circumstances. The same way friends will always tell you when there is spinach between your teeth, God points out specific areas that we need to address in order to move forward.

Who we allow to speak into our lives is important. True friends will invest and inject something into your life that will build you up and take you forward.

TWO ARE BETTER THAN ONE, BECAUSE THEY HAVE A GOO[D] REWARD FOR THEIR LABOUR. FOR IF THEY FALL, ONE W[ILL] LIFT UP HIS COMPANION. BUT WOE TO HIM WHO IS ALO[NE] WHEN HE FALLS, FOR HAS NO ONE TO HELP HIM U[P]. AGAIN, IF TWO LIE DOWN T[O]GETHER, THEY WILL KE[EP] WARM; BUT HOW CAN ONE BE WARM ALONE? THOUGH O[NE] MAY BE OVERPOWERED BY ANOTHER, TWO CAN WITHSTA[ND] HIM. AND A THREEFOLD CORD IS NOT QUICKLY BROKE[N].

> 'THERE IS A FRIEND WHO STICKS CLOSER THAN A BROTHER'
>
> [PROVERBS 18:24]

THE TEST OF FRIENDSHIP

When my two sons were growing up, they would fight each other (as brothers do) about petty things such as taking each other's socks. But they always stood up for each other if someone else was against them. There is a proverb that states:

'There is a friend who sticks closer than a brother' [Proverbs 18:24]

The kind of friendship that sticks closer than a brother is one that will endure anything. Not only will these friends be loyal and give you good counsel, but when the friendship is tested, they come through for you with flying colours.

Friendships like these should be highly prized and guarded. Trust is a key element in such relationships, yet trust isn't gained overnight. It is always sad when two people who have been life-long friends fall out. The Bible warns us about those things that can break friendships:

'*A whisperer separates the best of friends*' [Proverbs 16:28]

and

'*He who repeats a matter separates friends*' [Proverbs 17:9]

Your best friend may be privileged to know some intimate details about your life, but if he or she shared those secrets with another acquaintance, you would feel completely betrayed. Likewise, when one friend begins to entertain or meditate on the negative words of a third party, that small seed of doubt can begin to form a wedge in the relationship.

Guard your most precious relationships the same way you would guard your heart. Never take them for granted and be careful that you don't overstep the parameters.

Friendship is not a trivial relationship but adds to the fullness of a blessed life. I like the way Charles Swindoll said it, 'Let's face it, friends make life a lot more fun.'

Two are better than one, because they have a good

reward for their labour. For if they fall, one will

partnership

lift up his companion. But woe to him who is alone

when he falls. For he has no one to help him up.

Again, if two lie down together, they will keep warm;

THE POWER OF PARTNERSHIP

Two are better than one, because they have a good reward for their labour. For if they fall, one will lift up his companion. But woe to him who is alone when he falls, for he has no one to help him up. Again, if two lie down together, they will keep warm; but how can one be warm alone? Though one may be overpowered by another, two can withstand him. And a threefold cord is not quickly broken.

TWO ARE BETTER THAN ONE, BECAUSE THEY HAVE A GOOD REWARD FOR THEIR LABOUR. FOR IF THEY FALL, ONE WILL LIFT UP HIS COMPANION. BUT WOE TO HIM WHO IS ALONE WHEN HE FALLS, FOR HAS NO ONE TO HELP HIM UP. AGAIN, IF TWO LIE DOWN TOGETHER, THEY WILL KEEP WARM; BUT HOW CAN ONE BE WARM ALONE? THOUGH ONE MAY BE OVERPOWERED BY ANOTHER, TWO CAN WITHSTAND HIM. AND A THREEFOLD CORD IS NOT QUICKLY BROKEN

> 'TWO ARE BETTER THAN ONE'
>
> [ECCLESIASTES 4:9]

TWO ARE BETTER THAN ONE

Don't be fooled into thinking that you have the capacity to achieve your best on your own. A training partner in the gym is a great asset because when you think you have reached your limit, there is someone who can push you to go further.

Having someone who believes in you and encourages you to reach for your dream will add to your life and be a friend to your destiny. It was the blind and deaf Helen Keller who said, 'Alone we can do so little; together we can do so much.' The Bible puts it this way:

'Two are better than one' [Ecclesaistes 4:9]

This verse goes on to list the benefits of partnership and the blessings of intimacy. The desire to have intimate relationships is deep within every human being – be it with our life's partner, our family or close friendships.

To be 'intimate' means to be closely acquainted and familiar with someone else, and within the right parameters, intimacy is one of life's great blessings.

Yet to some, intimacy can become a curse. People who carry the scars of painful relationships can allow their past experiences to keep sabotaging their present and future relationships. To protect themselves, some put up walls to prevent others becoming too close to them. Others habitually form intimate relationships with the wrong people for the wrong reasons. To them, intimacy means confusion and pain.

Instead, intimacy should enhance and bless lives. If you have been hurt or betrayed by someone, don't allow that to prevent you from building good relationships in the future. A good starting point is becoming part of a local church that inspires you to expand and grow, building relationships with others whose lives are based on Bible principles.

TWO ARE BETTER THAN ONE, BECAUSE THEY HAVE A GO

REWARD FOR THEIR LABOUR.   FOR IF THEY FALL, ONE W

LIFT UP HIS COMPANION. BUT WOE TO HIM WHO IS ALO

WHEN   HE   FALLS, FOR

> 'THEY HAVE A GOOD REWARD FOR THEIR LABOUR'
>
> [ECCLESIASTES 4:9]

HAS NO ONE   TO HELP HIM

AGAIN, IF TWO   LIE DOWN T

GETHER, THEY   WILL   KE

WARM; BUT HOW CAN ONE BE WARM ALONE? THOUGH O

MAY BE OVERPOWERED BY ANOTHER, TWO CAN WITHSTA

HIM. AND A THREEFOLD CORD IS NOT QUICKLY BROKE

GREATER IMPACT AND SUPPORT

You have probably heard the saying, 'Many hands make light work.' What this implies is that teamwork gets a job done faster than one person can.

'Two are better than one, because they have a good reward for their labour.' [Ecclesiastes 4:9]

Working together enables you to have a greater impact and higher productivity. If you single-handedly tackle a task, such as building a brick wall, it will take considerably longer than two people working together. The reward for the work of two is far greater.

For example, the world's great airlines have formed alliances for the greater benefit of all involved. The reward of good partnerships and relationships is that they make us more effective and fruitful.

'Be fruitful and multiply' was the first command God gave to humanity. Being fruitful and multiplying isn't only about a man and a woman being physically intimate with each other and conceiving children. His will for our lives is that we increase and expand in everything we do. For instance, when we work together in unity, we can achieve so much more and have a greater influence and impact.

Besides achieving more together, two are better than one because you have assistance and support when you need it.

For if they fall, one will lift up his companion. But woe to him who is alone when he falls, for he has no one to help him up. [Ecclesiastes 4:10]

Your intimate friendships and relationships are the ones that will carry you through the hard times and celebrate the good times with you. When you face tough situations in life, those closest to you are the ones who support you by lifting you up when you are down.

TWO ARE BETTER THAN ONE, BECAUSE THEY HAVE A GO[OD]

REWARD FOR THEIR LABOUR. FOR IF THEY FALL, ONE W[ILL]

LIFT UP HIS COMPANION. BUT WOE TO HIM WHO IS ALO[NE]

WHEN HE FALLS, FOR [HE]

HAS NO ONE TO HELP HIM [UP.]

AGAIN, IF TWO LIE DOWN T[O-]

GETHER, THEY WILL KE[EP]

WARM; BUT HOW CAN ONE BE WARM ALONE? THOUGH O[NE]

MAY BE OVERPOWERED BY ANOTHER, TWO CAN WITHSTA[ND]

HIM. AND A THREEFOLD CORD IS NOT QUICKLY BROKE[N]

> 'THOUGH ONE MAY BE OVERPOWERED BY ANOTHER, TWO CAN WITHSTAND HIM'
>
> [ECCLESIASTES 4:10]

COMPANIONSHIP AND STRENGTH

'Two are better than one' is not only a principle that gives you greater impact and support, but also gives you the warmth of companionship and added strength when you are vulnerable.

Again, if two lie down together, they will keep warm; But how can one be warm alone? [Ecclesiastes 4: 11]

The warmth of a loving, close relationship is one of life's great blessings. It means having someone who rejoices with you when you have reason to celebrate, and who weeps with you when you are in pain. Such intimate relationships add warmth to your life.

Many mistakenly think that sex will produce the intimacy they crave, but outside God's parameters, sex can cause hurt and pain. Many extra-marital affairs aren't as much about lust as they are about the desire to fill that cold, empty void that comes from a lack of intimacy.

The power of two also provides strength and protection.

'*Though one may be overpowered by another, two can withstand him.*' [Ecclesiastes 4: 12]

When you stand alone, you are more likely to be overpowered, but when people stand together, it is a much more powerful force.

A breakdown in a marriage, a friendship or a team is often started by a wedge provided by a third party who introduces a small seed of doubt. Entertaining thoughts such as imagining you should be somewhere else or with another partner could take you down a path that leads to devastation.

Always remember that the devil's desire is to see strong relationships fail and if he can put a wedge into those partnerships, he will. Yet, in relationships that know genuine closeness and intimacy, any opening for interference by any other third party is firmly closed.

TWO ARE BETTER THAN ONE, BECAUSE THEY HAVE A GO[OD]
REWARD FOR THEIR LABOUR. FOR IF THEY FALL, ONE W[ILL]
LIFT UP HIS COMPANION. BUT WOE TO HIM WHO IS ALO[NE]
WHEN HE FALLS, FOR [HE]
HAS NO ONE TO HELP HIM [UP.]
AGAIN, IF TWO LIE DOWN T[O]
GETHER, THEY WILL KE[EP]
WARM; BUT HOW CAN ONE BE WARM ALONE? THOUGH O[NE]
MAY BE OVERPOWERED BY ANOTHER, TWO CAN WITHSTA[ND]
HIM. AND A THREEFOLD CORD IS NOT QUICKLY BROKE[N]

> 'AND A THREE-FOLD CORD IS NOT QUICKLY BROKEN'
>
> [ECCLESIASTES 4:12]

A THREE-FOLD CORD

During the Second World War, various nations formed an alliance against Nazi Germany. Their common enemy was the reason for the alliance. Whether it is a common goal, a shared vision or cause, or even a common enemy, every relationship has a third factor that binds them together. The Bible states:

'And a threefold cord is not quickly broken.' [Ecclesiastes 4:12]

Every partnership has three strands – firstly, there is you; secondly, there are those you are in partnership with, and the third part of the equation is the common interest that holds relationships together. It is this third cord that determines the impact of the partnership.

If you examine the various relationships in your life, you should be able to identify what holds them together. The uniting force of this third element is therefore very important because it determines whether that relationship will be healthy or unhealthy.

The things that unite people are diverse, and can be positive or negative. Bitterness and negativity can bring people together with destructive consequences.

'Pilate and Herod became friends with each other, for previously they had been at enmity with each other.' [Luke 23:12]

This verse describes two men who previously disliked each other but a shared contempt for Jesus became the third cord that tied their relationship together. When individuals leave a church, a sports club or workplace with a negative or critical spirit, they invariably find others who have shared a similar experience. Their similar attitude or mutual hurt becomes the cord that brings them together.

The most powerful cord is love. The Bible says that love never fails. When love is the primary force that binds a relationship together, there may be challenges, but the partnership will not be broken. The key to great relationships is to build the right third cord into partnerships that will prove indestructible.

TWO ARE BETTER THAN ONE, BECAUSE THEY HAVE A GO[OD]

REWARD FOR THEIR LABOUR. FOR IF THEY FALL, ONE W[ILL]

LIFT UP HIS COMPANION. BUT WOE TO HIM WHO IS ALO[NE]

WHEN HE FALLS, FOR [HE]

HAS NO ONE TO HELP HIM [UP.]

AGAIN, IF TWO LIE DOWN T[O-]

GETHER, THEY WILL KE[EP]

WARM; BUT HOW CAN ONE BE WARM ALONE? THOUGH O[NE]

MAY BE OVERPOWERED BY ANOTHER, TWO CAN WITHSTA[ND]

HIM. AND A THREEFOLD CORD IS NOT QUICKLY BROK[EN]

> 'THAT YOU BE PERFECTLY
> JOINED TOGETHER
> IN THE SAME MIND AND
> IN THE SAME JUDGEMENT'
>
> [1 CORINTHIANS 1:10]

PARTNERING FOR SUCCESS

Have you ever watched a couple on the dance floor who know how to move exceptionally well together? They blend into one with perfect rhythm and symmetry, and are irresistible to watch.

That is how God intends our partnerships and relationships to be. The Apostle Paul taught about unity and partnership, saying:

'That you all speak the same thing, and that there be no divisions among you, but that you be perfectly joined together in the same mind and in the same judgement.' [1 Corinthians 1:10]

A partnership is an alliance or unified force, with a shared purpose or a common interest. Partners in business share the risk, the costs, the consequences and ultimately share the profits. In a healthy marriage, partners share the bed, share their dreams, and share the blessing or assets of that marriage.

I believe there are things in your life that either attract or repel partnership. Many want the benefits, but aspects of their thinking, their personality or their lifestyle hold them back from building strong relationships.

There are those who were once in a partnership, be it a business or marriage relationship, that had disastrous results. They won't allow themselves to get involved again because of the pain and conflict they experienced.

Some think about partnership in selfish terms: 'Oh no, everything I have, I have to split in two.' But in successful partnerships, the rewards are multiplied. If you understand the power of genuinely sharing, it won't restrict you or mean that you have less. It will greatly enhance your life.

> 'JOINED AND KNIT TOGETHER BY WHAT EVERY JOINT SUPPLIES, ACCORDING TO THE EFFECTIVE WORKING BY WHICH EVERY PART DOES ITS SHARE'
>
> [EPHESIANS 4:16]

TWO ARE BETTER THAN ONE, BECAUSE THEY HAVE A GOOD REWARD FOR THEIR LABOUR. FOR IF THEY FALL, ONE WILL LIFT UP HIS COMPANION. BUT WOE TO HIM WHO IS ALONE WHEN HE FALLS, FOR HAS NO ONE TO HELP HIM AGAIN, IF TWO LIE DOWN TOGETHER, THEY WILL KEEP WARM; BUT HOW CAN ONE BE WARM ALONE? THOUGH ONE MAY BE OVERPOWERED BY ANOTHER, TWO CAN WITHSTAND HIM. AND A THREEFOLD CORD IS NOT QUICKLY BROKEN

SHARED CONTRIBUTION

A great relationship or partnership is like a two-way street – it involves shared contribution. To enjoy the blessing of partnership you have to put something *in* to get something *out*. Today we live in an instant society, where many want the immediate benefits, but they are not prepared for the hard work or cost to get there. They don't want to contribute or give anything, they only want to receive.

There are couples who may be husband and wife, yet never experience the power of partnership. Perhaps they don't understand the importance of being open and transparent with their spouse, so they make little intimate or emotional contribution to their relationship. Consequently they don't enjoy the blessing of partnership that God intends. It requires both parties to contribute to a relationship in order for it to succeed.

Similarly, you may attend a local church on a regular basis, but the blessing you experience will be determined by the level of your contribution and partnership in the vision. Those who are sacrificial in their contribution are those who take on the spirit of partnership and enjoy its full blessing.

Even those in leadership positions can miss the power of partnership. If they are insecure or threatened by others, they never see their team as partners and under-estimate their contribution. It is possible to have a large complement of staff who work for you or are around you, but fail to understand what it means to partner in the vision.

What is it like to have a team who does partner with you? If you want to know the blessing of partnership, you need to open yourself up and make your contribution into the lives of others.

TWO ARE BETTER THAN ONE, BECAUSE THEY HAVE A GO[OD]

REWARD FOR THEIR LABOUR. FOR IF THEY FALL, ONE W[ILL]

LIFT UP HIS COMPANION. BUT WOE TO HIM WHO IS ALO[NE]

WHEN HE FALLS, FOR [HE]

HAS NO ONE TO HELP HIM [UP].

AGAIN, IF TWO LIE DOWN T[O-]

GETHER, THEY WILL KE[EP]

WARM; BUT HOW CAN ONE BE WARM ALONE? THOUGH O[NE]

MAY BE OVERPOWERED BY ANOTHER, TWO CAN WITHSTA[ND]

HIM. AND A THREEFOLD CORD IS NOT QUICKLY BROKE[N]

> 'FOR I DO NOT MEAN
> THAT OTHERS SHOULD BE
> EASED AND YOU
> BURDENED; BUT BY AN
> EQUALITY'
>
> [2 CORINTHIANS 8:13]

SHARED EQUALITY

We are all equal in the eyes of God. He made us unique with different roles to fulfil, but that doesn't mean one is superior to another. Unfortunately there are those who distort what the Bible says about submission and so pervert the truth concerning Godly marriage and Godly leadership. They build their relationships on domination or control, and miss the real blessing of partnership that God intended.

Even though leadership will emerge in every relationship, Godly partnerships will enjoy equality. The Apostle Paul wrote:

*'For I do not mean that others should be eased and you burdened; but by an **equality**, that now at this time your abundance may supply their lack, that their abundance also may supply your lack—that there may be **equality**.'* [2 Corinthians 8:13,14]

Great partnerships are based on each one doing their share. In business, it is an unhealthy partnership if one person took all the risk and the other person enjoyed all the profit. Nor will a marriage be healthy if each one sees it in terms of their own interests. 'For richer, for poorer' doesn't mean you get richer and your partner gets poorer. Likewise, 'for better, for worse' doesn't mean better for you and worse for your partner.

Genuine equality understands what it means to be a blessing and brings a desire to empower your partner. If all you are interested in is how things affect you, you cannot experience the true spirit of partnership. A great partner recognises the risk and the cost, and is committed to carrying the share of the load ... and ultimately enjoys the shared blessing or reward.

TWO ARE BETTER THAN ONE, BECAUSE THEY HAVE A GO[OD] REWARD FOR THEIR LABOUR. FOR IF THEY FALL, ONE W[ILL] LIFT UP HIS COMPANION. BUT WOE TO HIM WHO IS ALO[NE] WHEN HE FALLS, FOR [HE] HAS NO ONE TO HELP HIM [UP.] AGAIN, IF TWO LIE DOWN T[O]GETHER, THEY WILL KE[EP] WARM; BUT HOW CAN ONE BE WARM ALONE? THOUGH O[NE] MAY BE OVERPOWERED BY ANOTHER, TWO CAN WITHSTA[ND] HIM. AND A THREEFOLD CORD IS NOT QUICKLY BROKE[N.]

> 'FOR WHEREVER YOU GO, I WILL GO'
>
> [RUTH 1:16]

SHARED COMMITMENT

Faithfulness and commitment are two more ingredients for a great partnership. There is a Proverb that says:

'Most men will proclaim each his own goodness, but who can find a faithful man?' [Proverbs 20:6]

The distinction is made between faithfulness and self-interest. The majority of people look out for their own interests, but a faithful person will have a sense of commitment that goes well beyond themselves.

Sadly, many are focused on their personal interests rather than putting the combined interests of the partnership first. Don't build your relationships according to the spirit of 'most men' – the attitude of the majority.

In the Old Testament, Ruth displayed an incredible spirit of commitment to her mother-in-law after they both lost their husbands. Instead of abandoning Naomi, this is what Ruth said:

'For wherever you go, I will go; And wherever you lodge, I will lodge; Your people shall be my people, and your God, my God. Where you die, I will die, and there will I be buried. The Lord do so to me, and more also, if anything but death parts you and me.'

[Ruth 1:16,17]

'Until death us do part' is a powerful commitment. Marriage partners may declare this in their wedding vows, but some never live at this level of commitment. There may be things your partner enjoys that you don't like doing, but why not do them willingly and allow their happiness to be your reward?

True commitment involves faithfulness towards the interests of your partner. Such commitment is the hallmark of a great partnership.

TWO ARE BETTER THAN ONE, BECAUSE THEY HAVE A GOOD REWARD FOR THEIR LABOUR. FOR IF THEY FALL, ONE WILL LIFT UP HIS COMPANION. BUT WOE TO HIM WHO IS ALONE WHEN HE FALLS, FOR HAS NO ONE TO HELP HIM UP. AGAIN, IF TWO LIE DOWN TOGETHER, THEY WILL KEEP WARM; BUT HOW CAN ONE BE WARM ALONE? THOUGH ONE MAY BE OVERPOWERED BY ANOTHER, TWO CAN WITHSTAND HIM. AND A THREEFOLD CORD IS NOT QUICKLY BROKEN

> 'WHO HAS SAVED AND CALLED US ACCORDING TO HIS OWN PURPOSE'
>
> [2 TIMOTHY 1:9]

SHARED PURPOSE

Ultimately, partnership is all about a shared purpose. When Hillsong Church made plans to build a new church building, there was a tremendous sense of rallying together as our congregation united to raise the finance. It was the shared purpose and committed partnership to the vision that enabled us to build our new facility.

It is often a sense of purpose or a cause that unites people in the first place. In business partnerships, the shared purpose may be profits. In a marriage, it could be the shared goals of building a family and a home.

Take a young couple who have a vision of building their own home and invest all their time and energy into their goal. They will see the reward of their labours but sadly, that shared purpose (third cord) can sometimes become the destructive element in their relationship. When the house is complete, they could discover there is nothing else between them when their common purpose is gone. Instead of sowing into their relationship, they invested too much into achieving their common goal.

In my book *For This Cause* I wrote about the power of partnering for the Cause of the King and the Kingdom. The Bible says:

'[He] *who has saved us and called us with a holy calling, not according to our works, but according to His own purpose.*'

[2 Timothy 1:9]

We are all alive for a specific purpose and a cause, and God will place other people in your life to help you achieve it. You will usually find people are drawn to those who have a sense of purpose. When you lose your sense of purpose, you tend to lose your sense of partnership as well.

It makes sense to examine the cords that are tying your partnerships together to see whether they will ultimately bring fulfilment or failure. Vision brings unity and unity brings reward.

Then the rib which the Lord God had taken from man He made into a woman,

and He brought her to the man. And Adam said: "This is now bone of my bones

marriage

and flesh of my flesh; She shall be called Woman, because she was taken out of

Man.' Therefore a man shall leave his father and mother and be joined to his

wife, and they shall become one flesh.

THE POWER OF MARRIAGE

Then the rib which the Lord God had taken from man He made into a woman, and He brought her to the man. And Adam said: 'This is now bone of my bones and flesh of my flesh; she shall be called Woman, because she was taken out of Man.' Therefore a man shall leave his father and mother and be joined to his wife, and they shall become one flesh.

TWO ARE BETTER THAN ONE, BECAUSE THEY HAVE A GO[OD]

REWARD FOR THEIR LABOUR. FOR IF THEY FALL, ONE W[ILL]

LIFT UP HIS COMPANION. BUT WOE TO HIM WHO IS ALO[NE]

WHEN HE FALLS, FOR [HE]

HAS NO ONE TO HELP HIM [UP]

AGAIN, IF TWO LIE DOWN T[O]

GETHER, THEY WILL KE[EP]

WARM; BUT HOW CAN ONE BE WARM ALONE? THOUGH O[NE]

MAY BE OVERPOWERED BY ANOTHER, TWO CAN WITHSTA[ND]

HIM. AND A THREEFOLD CORD IS NOT QUICKLY BROKE[N]

> 'AND THEY SHALL BECOME ONE'
>
> [GENESIS 2:24]

THE BLESSING OF MARRIAGE

I first met my wife Bobbie before her 17th birthday, and it was the beginning of a great God-ordained partnership that has enriched every area of my life. We've now been married for over 25 years and I can honestly testify that our marriage is stronger than ever. Is this a fluke? Are we just lucky? The truth is that choices have been made and the effort has been put into building a strong partnership.

'*He who finds a wife finds a good thing.*' [Proverbs 18:22]

Marriage is God's idea and He purposed it for good. It is the most intimate relationship you will have with another person because it is a powerful spiritual and physical union where two become one.

'*A man shall leave his mother and father, and be joined to his wife, and they shall become one.*' [Genesis 2: 24]

Being joined together describes being attached and connected. It literally means to stick like glue. Try to pull it apart and both parties will experience a lot of hurt and pain.

At the culmination of the marriage vows, the minister usually declares the words of Jesus over a couple:

'*Therefore **whom** God has joined together, let **no** man separate.*'

[Mark 10:9]

The fact is that you never want to pull apart what God has joined together, be it a marriage, or any other God-ordained partnership. On the other hand, you don't want to attempt to put together something that God never intended. Sadly, some people try and join things together that have no future, while others try to pull something apart that is very much part of God's plan.

One of the most significant choices we can ever make relates to the choice of our life partner, so we need to understand what it truly means to be joined together.

TWO ARE BETTER THAN ONE, BECAUSE THEY HAVE A GO[OD]

REWARD FOR THEIR LABOUR. FOR IF THEY FALL, ONE W[ILL]

LIFT UP HIS COMPANION. BUT WOE TO HIM WHO IS ALO[NE]

WHEN HE FALLS, FOR [HE]

HAS NO ONE **'DO NOT BE UNEQUALLY YOKED TO UNBELIEVERS'** TO HELP HIM

[2 CORINTHIANS 6:14]

AGAIN, IF TWO LIE DOWN T[O-]

GETHER, THEY WILL KE[EP]

WARM; BUT HOW CAN ONE BE WARM ALONE? THOUGH O[NE]

MAY BE OVERPOWERED BY ANOTHER, TWO CAN WITHSTA[ND]

HIM. AND A THREEFOLD CORD IS NOT QUICKLY BROK[EN]

MAKING RIGHT CHOICES

Choosing your marriage partner is one of the most important decisions you will ever make. Marriage is intended to be the greatest partnership in life, but when built on a poor foundation, it is doomed to struggle or fail.

There are several reasons why people choose the wrong partner – it can be a strong physical attraction, becoming involved on the rebound, or wanting to avoid being single at any cost. Ultimately, they ignore wise counsel and the warning signals. You can avoid making a serious mistake by considering these three key warning signs.

Watch out for spiritual compatibility – The Bible is clear that we should not be unequally yoked. When two lives are pulling in different directions, something has to give. There will obviously be a potential source of disagreement and such conflict won't help build a harmonious marriage. Sharing the same values, morals, ethics and spiritual beliefs is vital for a blessed partnership.

Be careful when there is emotional dysfunction – Don't ignore the signs of someone who has a pattern of extreme behaviour. Severe depression, hypersensitivity or problems such as bulimia are not suddenly going to disappear after you get married. We all have issues in life which need to be overcome but mistakes can be made because of what we ignore. For example, a cute smile will not mask an ugly temper. A marriage can be destroyed by emotional problems that haven't been dealt with.

Sexual perversion or confusion – Sex was created to bless a deeply intimate relationship between husband and wife, but outside God's parameters, it will only bring hurt and pain. Even when a person has turned away from their past experiences, it takes time to renew their thinking, and change old behaviour patterns to line up with the Word.

Both partners will reap what is sown into a marriage, so use Godly wisdom when it comes to a life-long partnership.

TWO ARE BETTER THAN ONE, BECAUSE THEY HAVE A GO

REWARD FOR THEIR LABOUR.   FOR IF THEY FALL, ONE W

LIFT UP HIS COMPANION. BUT WOE TO HIM WHO IS ALO

WHEN   HE   FALLS, FOR

HAS NO ONE   TO HELP HIM

AGAIN, IF TWO   LIE DOWN T

GETHER, THEY   WILL   KE

WARM; BUT HOW CAN ONE BE WARM ALONE? THOUGH O

MAY BE OVERPOWERED BY ANOTHER, TWO CAN WITHSTA

HIM. AND A THREEFOLD CORD IS NOT QUICKLY BROK

> 'BLESSED ARE
> THOSE WHOSE
> STRENGTH
> IS IN YOU'
>
> [PSALM 84:5]

THREE SECRETS FOR A STRONG MARRIAGE

From the moment a couple are joined together in marriage, they begin a journey of life together. Like any road travelled, there will inevitably be twists and turns to negotiate.

Every marriage has its share of tests and trials, but why do some emerge stronger, while others fall apart? I can testify to three key secrets that will help to build a strong marriage.

Two people who love God

Two people who love God and put Him first in their lives have the ingredient for a strong marriage. When one partner is passionate about God and His purpose but the other isn't, it makes the journey together a lot more difficult.

'Blessed is the man whose strength is in You.' [Psalm 84:5]

When the strength of your marriage is your commitment to Him, you can go through challenges and emerge stronger.

Two people who love the House of God

The Bible is clear that one of the keys to a blessed life is our association with God's House (His Church). It says:

'Those who are planted in God's House shall flourish' [Psalm 92:13]

'Blessed are those who dwell in Your House' [Psalm 84:4]

My personal experience is that the love Bobbie and I share for the Church has been a unifying factor in our marriage and the strength of our family.

Two people who love each other

It may seem obvious, but the third secret of a blessed marriage is a union of two people who love each other. This is the love that Paul wrote about in 1 Corinthians 13 – it suffers long, it is kind, and it does not envy or parade itself. This love doesn't seek its own, is not provoked and thinks no evil. It bears all things, believes all things, hopes all things and endures all things. This is a love that will 'never fail.'

TWO ARE BETTER THAN ONE, BECAUSE THEY HAVE A GO[OD]
REWARD FOR THEIR LABOUR. FOR IF THEY FALL, ONE W[ILL]
LIFT UP HIS COMPANION. BUT WOE TO HIM WHO IS ALO[NE]
WHEN   HE   FALLS, FOR [HE]
HAS NO ONE   TO HELP HIM [UP]
AGAIN, IF TWO   LIE DOWN T[O-]
GETHER, THEY   WILL   K[EEP]
WARM; BUT HOW CAN ONE BE WARM ALONE? THOUGH O[NE]
MAY BE OVERPOWERED BY ANOTHER, TWO CAN WITHSTA[ND]
HIM. AND A THREEFOLD CORD IS NOT QUICKLY BROK[EN]

> 'DO NOT TO LET
> THE SUN GO DOWN
> ON YOUR
> WRATH'
>
> [EPHESIANS 4:26]

BUILDING YOUR MARRIAGE DAY-TO-DAY

When a couple admits their marriage is in trouble, it is often the little everyday issues that have been suppressed for a long period of time that create most of the problems. The Bible gives us what may appear to be simple counsel, yet which can prevent these issues from sabotaging your future.

Resolve issues quickly

'Do not to let the sun go down on your wrath.' [Ephesians 4:26]

People allow the sun to go down on unforgiveness, resentment, hurt and regret. They carry around baggage from the past that eventually begins to rule their lives. Eventually, all their pent-up anger and their unresolved emotion pours out. Often they have left it until their relationship is irreparable.

The best advice is to deal with issues so that yesterday's pain is not determining the health of your marriage today. Jesus said, 'Sufficient for the day is its own trouble' but many cannot even confront today's challenges because of the junk still occupying them from the past.

Speak words of life

'Death and life are in the power of the tongue, and those who love it will eat its fruit.' [Proverbs 18:21]

Words bear fruit, positively or negatively – they can either build others up or be lethal weapons of devastation and damage. Whether spoken by you or over you, words have the power to affect your relationships. Thoughtless, careless words can mortally wound a marriage or scar a child for life.

Your words are like deposits in others that can ultimately shape their lives. Encouraging words of praise build confidence and self-worth, but constant criticism and disapproval produces a sense of failure and rejection. The Bible says, 'The lips of the righteous feed many' (Proverbs 10:21). Make a decision to speak words of life that will bless your partner and build them up.

> Two are better than one, because they have a good reward for their labour. For if they fall, one will lift up his companion. But woe to him who is alone when he falls, for he has no one to help him up. Again, if two lie down together, they will keep warm; but how can one be warm alone? Though one may be overpowered by another, two can withstand him. And a threefold cord is not quickly broken.

> 'But whoever desires to be become great among you, let him be a servant'
>
> [MATTHEW 20:26]

COMMITTED TO YOUR PARTNER'S SUCCESS

When Bobbie and I married, we had both lived in a relatively small world in New Zealand. Over the years I have enjoyed seeing her life grow and expand. Today she has increased in confidence and her gifts and talents have flourished. She has written books and speaks all over the world.

Sadly, there are those who keep their partner suppressed and shackled. Some even use scriptures out of context to control their spouse and keep their world small. Because of this insecurity, their home is full of resentment, hurt and negativity. The truth is that by holding your partner back, you also hold your own life back.

Learn to invest into your partner. Empowering them to become a bigger person will lead to greater horizons for you both. Most Christians recognise Proverbs 31 as depicting the awesome qualities of a Godly woman, but I think you also gain valuable insight into her marriage.

'She makes tapestry for herself; Her clothing is fine linen and purple. Her husband is known in the gates, when he sits among the elders of the land.' [Proverbs 31: 22,23]

This verse describes a man who is a well-known and influential leader whose wife is obviously able to dress in fine garments. But here is another way of looking at it – perhaps his commitment to dressing his wife in fine linen contributed towards his success.

I'm not talking about the expense of clothes or what people wear, but an attitude that loves blessing and empowering the people around you. If you can see beyond yourself and be committed to seeing your partner flourish, it can open you up to a much bigger, expansive life and build a wonderful marriage.

Our Father in Heaven. Hallowed be Your name. Your Kingdom come. Your

will be done on earth as it is in Heaven. Give us this day our daily bread.

family

And forgive us our debts, as we forgive our debtors. And do not lead us into

temptation, but deliver us from the evil one. For Yours is the kingdom and

the   power   and   the   glory   forever.   Amen.

THE POWER OF FAMILY

Our Father in Heaven, hallowed be Your name. Your Kingdom come. Your will be done on earth as it is in Heaven. Give us this day our daily bread. And forgive us our debts, as we forgive our debtors. And do not lead us into temptation, but deliver us from the evil one. For Yours is the kingdom and the power and the glory forever. Amen.

TWO ARE BETTER THAN ONE, BECAUSE THEY HAVE A GO[OD]

REWARD FOR THEIR LABOUR. FOR IF THEY FALL, ONE W[ILL]

LIFT UP HIS COMPANION. BUT WOE TO HIM WHO IS ALO[NE]

WHEN HE FALLS, FOR [HE]

HAS NO ONE TO HELP HIM [UP.]

> 'CHILDREN
> ARE A HERITAGE
> FROM THE LORD'
>
> [PSALM 127:3]

AGAIN, IF TWO LIE DOWN T[O-]

GETHER, THEY WILL KE[EP]

WARM; BUT HOW CAN ONE BE WARM ALONE? THOUGH O[NE]

MAY BE OVERPOWERED BY ANOTHER, TWO CAN WITHSTA[ND]

HIM. AND A THREEFOLD CORD IS NOT QUICKLY BROKE[N]

THE BLESSING OF CHILDREN

I will never forget the day I became a father for the first time. I ran towards my car in the parking lot of St Margaret's hospital in Sydney with an incredible sense of elation. I had a son – I was a Dad!

I'll also never forget the second time I became a father – or the third time – because words cannot describe the wonderful experience of becoming a parent. It changes your perspective on life forever. Suddenly the concept of 'family' takes on a whole new meaning.

Someone once said that the family you come from isn't as important as the family you are going to have. When you were born, you were part of someone else's family, but when you become a parent, you create a new family – and with that comes the responsibility of looking after them.

Family, like marriage, is God's idea. The Bible says:

'Children are a heritage from the Lord.' [Psalm 127:3]

What an incredible gift we are entrusted with – the lives of a new generation. There is no parent on the entire planet who has never made a mistake in their parenting. There is also no sane parent who looked at a newborn child and deliberately intended to mess their life up. The great thing is that the Bible contains a wealth of wisdom and counsel that equips us to raise our children to live life successfully.

Jesus said that our Father in Heaven knows the things we have need of before we ask Him (Matthew 6:8). As parents, our challenge is to know the needs of our children and invest the right ingredients into building their lives.

TWO ARE BETTER THAN ONE, BECAUSE THEY HAVE A GO[OD] REWARD FOR THEIR LABOUR. FOR IF THEY FALL, ONE W[ILL] LIFT UP HIS COMPANION. BUT WOE TO HIM WHO IS ALO[NE] WHEN HE FALLS, FOR [HE] HAS NO ONE TO HELP HIM U[P.] AGAIN, IF TWO LIE DOWN T[O-] GETHER, THEY WILL KE[EP] WARM; BUT HOW CAN ONE BE WARM ALONE? THOUGH O[NE] MAY BE OVERPOWERED BY ANOTHER, TWO CAN WITHSTA[ND] HIM. AND A THREEFOLD CORD IS NOT QUICKLY BROKE[N.]

> 'OUR FATHER IN HEAVEN,
> HALLOWED BE YOUR NAME
> YOUR KINGDOM COME
> YOUR WILL BE DONE ON
> EARTH AS IT IS IN HEAVEN'
>
> [MATTHEW 6: 9-11]

GIVING YOUR CHILDREN YOUR BEST

The Lord's Prayer is a wonderful example of a Son communicating with His Father and within this prayer, I have discovered some wonderful advice about what I can give my children.

A good name

'Our Father in Heaven, hallowed be Your Name.' [Matthew 6: 9]

My wife chose to adopt my name when we got married but our children inherited my name when they were born. A name is something they should be able to wear with honour, not a liability that brings shame. Give your children a name with which they can hold their heads up high.

A relationship with God

'Your will be done on earth as it is in Heaven.' [Matthew 6: 10]

Children will always bring you down to earth, so it is important to be relatable and allow them to be real. Some parents try and take earth to Heaven by demanding that their children be little angels. Instead we need to take the things of Heaven and apply them to earth, allowing our children to see the testimony of God working in our lives. Train them in the ways of God in a relatable manner that equips them to love God and love life. Help them to see that the will of God is exciting and can be applied to the real world.

Being a breadwinner

'Give us this day our daily bread.' [Matthew 6: 11]

My kids certainly know where to come when they need money ... and I don't mind that. Yet being the breadwinner is far more than simply providing for the family's material needs. It includes the responsibility to teach them to tap into the resource of Heaven for themselves, and to equip them with the wisdom, understanding and knowledge to live resourcefully, and to know the benefits of hard work, consistency and generosity.

TWO ARE BETTER THAN ONE, BECAUSE THEY HAVE A GO[OD]

REWARD FOR THEIR LABOUR. FOR IF THEY FALL, ONE W[ILL]

LIFT UP HIS COMPANION. BUT WOE TO HIM WHO IS ALO[NE]

WHEN HE FALLS, FOR [HE]

HAS NO ONE TO HELP HIM

AGAIN, IF TWO LIE DOWN T[O]

GETHER, THEY WILL KE[EP]

WARM; BUT HOW CAN ONE BE WARM ALONE? THOUGH O[NE]

MAY BE OVERPOWERED BY ANOTHER, TWO CAN WITHSTA[ND]

HIM. AND A THREEFOLD CORD IS NOT QUICKLY BROKE[N]

> 'DO NOT LEAD US INTO TEMPTATION BUT DELIVER US FROM THE EVIL ONE'
>
> [MATTHEW 6:12-13]

YOUR RELATIONSHIP WITH YOUR CHILDREN

God as a father gives us a pattern for the kind of relationship we can build with our children that will positively influence their lives.

Be a friend

'Forgive us our debts as we forgive our debtors.' [Matthew 6:12]

One of the great challenges is not only to be a parent, but also to be a friend to your children. Some parents never give their children room to grow and never forgive them for their shortcomings. Instead of forcing them to become what *you* want them to be, accept them for who they are and let them be who they are destined to be.

Be a leader

'Do not lead us into temptation.' [Matthew 6:13]

Where are you leading your children? Is your example leading your children into temptation to rebel in life?

Leadership is about example, and the example you set is the example they will follow. You cannot successfully be a parent who says, 'Do what I say but not what I do.'

Be a coach or trainer

'Deliver us from the evil one.' [Matthew 6:13]

A good coach is one who encourages sports players in their strengths and helps them to overcome their weaknesses in order to be successful.

As parents, we have the opportunity to shape the lives of our children and equip them with positive life skills. Sadly, there are those who haven't been coached to live life well. Perhaps you were raised by an austere parent who was always critical and didn't know how to give or receive love. Yet we can deliver our children from the clutches of poor examples of the past and coach them to be overcomers through exemplifying the way they should go. The way we think is passed down through generations and our responsibility is to train up our children to live a blessed life.

TWO ARE BETTER THAN ONE, BECAUSE THEY HAVE A GO[OD]

REWARD FOR THEIR LABOUR.   FOR IF THEY FALL, ONE W[ILL]

LIFT UP HIS COMPANION. BUT WOE TO HIM WHO IS ALO[NE]

WHEN HE FALLS, FOR [HE]

HAS NO ONE TO HELP HIM [UP.]

AGAIN, IF TWO LIE DOWN T[O-]

GETHER, THEY WILL KE[EP]

WARM; BUT HOW CAN ONE BE WARM ALONE? THOUGH O[NE]

MAY BE OVERPOWERED BY ANOTHER, TWO CAN WITHSTA[ND]

HIM. AND A THREEFOLD CORD IS NOT QUICKLY BROKE[N.]

> 'TRAIN UP A CHILD
> IN THE WAY HE
> SHOULD GO AND
> WHEN HE IS OLD,
> HE WILL NOT
> DEPART FROM IT'
>
> [PROVERBS 22:6]

TRAINING CHILDREN UP

The Bible says that if you train up children in the way they should go, they will not depart from it when they are old. The flipside of that scripture applies as well. If you train up children in the way they shouldn't go, they will not easily depart from that way either.

For instance, you may have grown up with a battler mentality and are unable to comprehend any other way of living except by struggling financially. That's the way your parents thought and so you were trained to think that way too.

Today there is a trend to target parents as the source of blame for your own failures in life. While it may be necessary to identify where your behaviour originated, this is no excuse or reason to stay that way.

No matter what your upbringing was, you can change the future generations by becoming a wise parent to your children. The Bible contains some excellent keys for investing into the lives of children and training them up in the way they should go.

Godly discipline

> *'Discipline your son, and he will give you peace; he will bring delight to your soul.'* [Proverbs 29:17]

The key to discipline is *consistency*, rather than lashing out when you lose your temper. If you are consistent about what you do and say, you will raise great children.

Love them, but don't spoil them

> *'If a man pampers his servant from youth, he will bring grief in the end.'* [Proverbs 29: 21]

There is a vast difference between loving and spoiling your children. Remember that love will include chastening your child when need be. Every child needs to know that every action has a consequence (or as the Bible puts it – we reap what we sow.)

TWO ARE BETTER THAN ONE, BECAUSE THEY HAVE A GO[OD] REWARD FOR THEIR LABOUR. FOR IF THEY FALL, ONE W[ILL] LIFT UP HIS COMPANION. BUT WOE TO HIM WHO IS ALO[NE] WHEN HE FALLS, FOR [HE] HAS NO ONE TO HELP HIM [UP]. AGAIN, IF TWO LIE DOWN T[O]GETHER, THEY WILL KE[EP] WARM; BUT HOW CAN ONE BE WARM ALONE? THOUGH O[NE] MAY BE OVERPOWERED BY ANOTHER, TWO CAN WITHSTA[ND] HIM. AND A THREEFOLD CORD IS NOT QUICKLY BROKE[N]

> 'WHERE THERE IS NO VISION, THE PEOPLE PERISH'
>
> [PROVERBS 29:18]

INVESTING INTO YOUR CHILDREN

Children who grow up hearing 'You're hopeless' or 'You'll never amount to anything' inevitably tend to believe it. The words you speak are powerful, and what you say will influence and impact the lives of your children.

Live by Godly principles

'Blessed is he who keeps the Word.' [Proverbs 29:18]

Previously I mentioned the importance of setting an example for your children to follow and to train them up in the way they should go. Living by Bible principles means you will see Bible results. Telling your children that they should 'honour their father and mother' is more powerful when they see how you honour your parents.

Fill their lives with vision

'Where there is no vision, the people cast off restraint.' [Proverbs 29:18]

You cannot ignore the link between rebellion and lack of a vision. Without purpose, there is a sense of hopelessness and people begin to live carelessly. Encourage your children to reach for their dreams and you will give them direction and purpose in life.

Take responsibility for a peaceful home

'An angry man stirs up dissension, and a hot-tempered one commits many sins.' [Proverbs 29: 22]

Take responsibility for creating the atmosphere of your home. Peace is often the same word used for 'prosperity' in the Bible, and by keeping an even temper, your family will enjoy the blessing of a happy home.

Be humble

'A man's pride brings him low, but a man of lowly spirit gains honour.' [Proverbs 29: 23]

Have you ever said 'sorry' to your children? Pride will always bring devastation, and many families have been devastated by the inability of parents to confront their own mistakes. Transparency and honesty are invaluable.

Love suffers long and is kind; love does not envy; love does not

parade itself, is not puffed up; does not behave rudely; does not seek

relationships

its own; is not provoked; thinks no evil; does not rejoice in

iniquity, but rejoices in the truth; bears all things, believes all things,

hopes all things, endures all things. Love never fails.

BUILDING GREAT
RELATIONSHIPS

Love suffers long and is kind; love does not envy; love does not parade itself, is not puffed up; does not behave rudely; does not seek its own; is not provoked; thinks no evil; does not rejoice in iniquity, but rejoices in the truth; bears all things, believes all things, hopes all things, endures all things. Love never fails.

TWO ARE BETTER THAN ONE, BECAUSE THEY HAVE A GO[OD] REWARD FOR THEIR LABOUR. FOR IF THEY FALL, ONE W[ILL] LIFT UP HIS COMPANION. BUT WOE TO HIM WHO IS ALO[NE] WHEN HE FALLS, FOR HAS NO ONE TO HELP HIM [UP.] AGAIN, IF TWO LIE DOWN T[O]GETHER, THEY WILL KE[EP] WARM; BUT HOW CAN ONE BE WARM ALONE? THOUGH O[NE] MAY BE OVERPOWERED BY ANOTHER, TWO CAN WITHSTA[ND] HIM. AND A THREEFOLD CORD IS NOT QUICKLY BROKE[N]

> 'SEEK FIRST THE KINGDOM OF GOD AND HIS RIGHTEOUSNESS AND ALL THESE THINGS SHALL BE ADDED TO YOU'
>
> [MATTHEW 6:33]

PRIORITIES FOR GREAT RELATIONSHIPS

A great marriage and family, as well as friendships and partnerships, are built on putting them first in your life. Give them second place and you will have second-rate relationships.

The reality is, if you want great relationships, you will need to make them a priority. Jesus teaches us three priorities for our relationships – the things that should come first.

'First be reconciled to your brother' [Matthew 5:24]

If you have a fallout in a close intimate relationship, it is important to work towards reconciliation. Holding on to bitterness and anger can rule and impact every aspect of your life. The Bible instructs us to 'pursue peace' (Hebrews 12:14) so whether it is with family, a work colleague or a friend, get your relationships in order. Some destructive relationships need to be severed completely, but settle them quickly and move on.

'First remove the plank from your own eye' [Matthew 7:5]

Human nature tends to see what is wrong with others more easily than seeing what needs changing within themself. Instead of being judgemental and critical, learn to live with a positive, encouraging spirit towards others. Don't be harsh in your thinking but rather believe the best in people. Why not give them the benefit of the doubt?

'Sit down first and count the cost' [Luke 14:28]

Jesus taught us how to count the cost before we begin anything. As a friend, how far will you go to help someone in need? As a partner, are you prepared to ride the challenges that come your way? As a parent, can you love your children no matter what they do?

There will always be obstacles to face in all your relationships, but if you have evaluated the cost beforehand, you can go the distance.

TWO ARE BETTER THAN ONE, BECAUSE THEY HAVE A GO[OD]

REWARD FOR THEIR LABOUR. FOR IF THEY FALL, ONE W[ILL]

LIFT UP HIS COMPANION. BUT WOE TO HIM WHO IS ALO[NE]

WHEN HE FALLS, FOR [HE]

HAS NO ONE TO HELP HIM U[P]

AGAIN, IF TWO LIE DOWN T[O]

GETHER, THEY WILL KE[EP]

WARM; BUT HOW CAN ONE BE WARM ALONE? THOUGH O[NE]

MAY BE OVERPOWERED BY ANOTHER, TWO CAN WITHSTA[ND]

HIM. AND A THREEFOLD CORD IS NOT QUICKLY BROKE[N]

> '... THAT I MAY KNOW HIM'
>
> [PHILIPPIANS 3:10]

FRIENDS FAMILY FAITH

In February 2002 Bobbie and I celebrated 25 years of marriage, surrounded by the wonderful family and friends God has placed in our lives. The glory of that milestone in our journey goes to God.

Psalm 84 describes the blessing of God on those whose strength is in Him, 'whose hearts are set on pilgrimage' (Psalm 84:5). Our marriage, family and friendships have all been set on the journey we travel together in faith, committed to the Cause of Christ.

On the wall of the main reception foyer of our church are the words 'Friends Family Faith' in bold letters. These words encapsulate the healthy relationships that contribute to the healthy, functional church we are today. Essentially, we are all part of a very big family – the family of God. The Bible says:

'The Lord puts the solitary in families.' [Psalm 68:6]

One of the signs of a prosperous life is healthy relationships and the Word of God gives us the principles we need to build them. When you recognise that the Bible contains the keys to building great relationships across the spectrum of your life, you will begin to tap into the blessing God has for you.

One cannot put a value on great relationships. They don't come by chance but sowing or investing into others will reap the highest rewards.

May all your relationships go from strength to strength.

x x

BOOKS BY BRIAN HOUSTON

GET A LIFE
PRINCIPLES FOR SUCCESS AND ENJOYMENT
IN EVERY AREA OF LIFE

YOU NEED MORE MONEY
DISCOVERING GOD'S AMAZING FINANCIAL PLAN
FOR YOUR LIFE

YOU CAN CHANGE THE FUTURE
LIVING BEYOND TODAY AND IMPACTING
THE GENERATIONS AHEAD

FOR THIS CAUSE
FINDING THE MEANING OF LIFE, AND
LIVING A LIFE OF MEANING

BOOKS BY BOBBIE HOUSTON

I'LL HAVE WHAT SHE'S HAVING
THE ULTIMATE COMPLIMENT TO ANY WOMAN DARING TO
LOOK LIFE IN THE FACE

HEAVEN IS IN THIS HOUSE

THE MAXIMISED LIFE SERIES

FURTHER TITLES IN THIS SERIES

HOW TO LIVE A BLESSED LIFE
PRINCIPLES FROM THE LIFE OF
THE RIGHTEOUS MAN IN PSALM 112

HOW TO MANAGE YOUR LIFE
PRINCIPLES FOR EVERY DECADE OF LIFE

HOW TO LIVE IN HEALTH AND HEALING
PRINCIPLES FOR A HEALTHY LIFESTYLE

HOW TO BE EMPLOYED, PROSPEROUS AND HAPPY
PRINCIPLES FOR ENJOYING WORK AND
REAPING THE BENEFITS

HOW TO EMPOWER THE WOMEN IN YOUR LIFE
PRINCIPLES FOR RELEASING WOMEN TO
REACH THEIR POTENTIAL

For more information on resource material
by Brian and Bobbie Houston, contact:
Maximised Leadership
PO Box 1195, Castle Hill NSW Australia 1765
www.maximisedleadership.com

YOUR RELATIONSHIP WITH GOD

It is impossible to write a book on building great relationships without mentioning the most important relationship of all – your relationship with God. Many people *know about* God, but they miss the blessing of *knowing Him* personally. Some never know that they can. Sadly, many spend their lives running from Him, not realising that they can have a personal relationship with the One who is committed to seeing them succeed in every area of life.

Your relationship with God has the power to impact every other relationship you have. Once you know Him, every other relationship has the added potential to be a success and a blessing.

God created us to know the blessing of intimacy – to have close fellowship and a personal relationship with Him. It was never His intention to have robotic creatures that He could control from Heaven, like puppets on a string.

The original intentions of God for mankind are described in the book of Genesis. Not only did He give Adam and Eve everything they could ever want or need, but they had an intimate relationship with Him, walking and talking with Him in the perfection of creation. It was only after they disregarded God's command not to eat from the tree of good and evil that they hid from Him, and sin became the great rift in the relationship between God and humanity.

This is where the awesome unconditional love God has for us is revealed. Whereas man was responsible for breaking the relationship with God, God took responsibility for restoring His relationship with man. He sent His most precious possession – His Son, Jesus – to bring reconciliation. That's the Gospel in a nutshell – acknowledging who Jesus is and what He did enables every one of us to have that wonderful, intimate relationship with God again.

TWO ARE BETTER THAN ONE, BECAUSE THEY HAVE A GOOD REWARD FOR THEIR LABOUR. FOR IF THEY FALL, ONE WILL LIFT UP HIS COMPANION. BUT WOE TO HIM WHO IS ALONE WHEN HE FALLS, FOR HE HAS NO ONE TO HELP HIM UP. AGAIN, IF TWO LIE DOWN TOGETHER, THEY WILL KEEP WARM; BUT HOW CAN ONE BE WARM ALONE? THOUGH ONE MAY BE OVERPOWERED BY ANOTHER, TWO CAN WITHSTAND HIM. AND A THREEFOLD CORD IS NOT QUICKLY BROKEN.

Brian and Bobbie Houston celebrating their 25th wedding anniversary with the Hillsong Church staff [February 2002]